# STRANDS

# STRANDS

*Keri Hulme*

AUCKLAND UNIVERSITY PRESS

First published 1992
Auckland University Press
Private Bag 92019
Auckland, New Zealand

ISBN 1 86940 068 2

Typeset by Deadline Typesetting
Printed by University Printing Services

Distributed outside New Zealand by Oxford University Press

Publication is assisted by the Literature Committee of the
Queen Elizabeth II Arts Council.

# CONTENTS

# ACKNOWLEDGEMENTS

'Lullaby for a Stone Doll' and 'Deity Considered as Mother Death' were first published in the *Mothers* catalogue (The Women's Gallery, Wellington, 1981); 'He Hoha' appeared in *Into the World of Light*, edited by W. Ihimaera and D. Long (Heinemann, 1982); 'Pauashell Gods' in *Landfall* 37 (1983); 'Waiting on the Laughing Owl' in *Poetry New Zealand* 6 (McIndoe, 1985), while 'Winesong 23' first saw light of day in *Yellow Pencils*, edited by L. Wevers (OUP, 1988).

## Dedication

Ki te whanau, tenei koha —

I brought a bottle filled with West Coast rain
and the newest leaf from my tree
to show I cherish
then and now, thee again

       still thee

Words mean
precisely what you want to hear them say
exactly
what you see in them

# 1

## FISHING
## THE OLEARIA TREE

---

Watch trees
stand in threes
eyes to the outer side —

The lagoon is on the maps. Stars fall into its waters: wounded
fish shelter there. People live on its margins, and crabs. Boats
drift across the water-top, and over all, the birds —

You grow with the stories and the stories say:
a bird from the other side, the twelfth heaven,
a bird which left reality with Rehua and now flies,
its own shadow, between here and hereafter

you get hints and shadows of the pattern but never
a complete and steady sighting.

The royal spoonbill is here, really a beak with a bird
attached, kotuku-ngutupapa as the naming goes, 'a bare
black face and baleful yellow eyelids'. The little shag is here,
dancing clown attendance. And in August, the others come.

The lagoon is on the maps. The others build nests and rear
their chicks from bluish-green eggs, all the while elegant themselves
in dorsal aigrettes, nuptial plumage. They are not
many: the survivor chicks are also few.

We dreamed we won the land . . .
now we wake, and know
the land won us a long long time
an age ago.

It stands, a yard of bird in its adult pride. The family is flown
throughout the land: here the strangers, in green squeaking flocks
flutter and glean and ripen all autumn.

The heron is perched on my roof. It is crouched against the
wind, the precision feathering blown awry, crowded into
sharp-edged ridges. The heron stares with a cold eye at the
blood by its feet. The blood is from a shot possum. It would
affect the heron no more no less if it came from me.

I bury the carcass in the compost pit — taihoa
calling it carcass brutalises both:
a corpse is a corpse is a corpse
— I mean, god help us all if I start looking on the world
with a heron's eye.

The Chatham Islands olearia tree feeds well from the pit. It
stands twelve feet tall now, grown from the mere bush of five
years back. Yes, that tree is truly on the map.

The lagoon is under my roof.

The birdwoman hunts the lagoon. She stalks us all with her
    yard-long ivory nails.
She continues, hungry, you know the end
in your back, sudden as the heron's bill
exact through the water-top — you thought
you were safe in this air of reality?
She snaps through the crack, you are not Hatupatu, you do
    not escape.

The tree holds up my roof:
I have these things on my tree;
a paper kite in the shape of a tropic dragonfly
such as Chinese children flew;
a barometer shaped like a porthole in brass & glass
such as old ships never carried;
borer holes, much greenery, and a crucifix the spiders
have nearly succeeded in shrouding.
It is made of some dark foreign wood, and the corpus is silver.
The nails in the hands got lost in an earthquake.
I replaced them long ago with chitonous slivers I carved from a feather.
Highly symbolic, for me, at the time.

     'For that which befalleth humanity, befalleth beasts;
     as one dieth, so dieth the other . . . so that no one
     hath pre-eminence above a beast.'

Ahh, Ecclesiastes: we dreamed
                    you get hints
                    there are maps.

(You take a black path to my house
— that fantail flicking     there
                        there
here     knows it.)

1:7     A dozen shags in a line, making themselves a living net
        fishing silveries on the bridge corner
        where the flax bushes tilt into the tide.

2:7     The sea very calm, motionless except for the sun glitter.
        A Caspian tern upset about something and
            scolding everything in sight
        — sun gulls bushes other taranui sea me.

3:7     There are five grey mallards over on the island shores,
        heads folded back tucked by wings, breasts uptilted
        soaking in the sun.

5:7     The sun is a pale smudge-edged disk. Sandflies
            swarm all over
        the window, a winter hatch

                    fresh & hungry the new brood
                    humming hunting for opportune flesh
                    view hallooo! aa blood ho ho!
                    hail little sister — here, drink your fill
                    — and now, to squash you —

        The sky exceedingly grey, except for cumulus
            clouds towering
        huge and scalloped and pallid on the horizon.

11

The wind gets up. The waxeyes in tiny shrieking flocks are
skidding wildly through the air. I see the heron in the
distance/aloof/beyond the wind's cold chant.

    I walk
    the muttering rustling shingle
    and the flat grey sea hissing on the stones
    I watch

        keep your eyes to the outer side
        never dream blind
        or your bones'll mingle —

The black rocks are under my roof, away in the tenebrous tide.

Somebody's been planting
godpoles on the beach: they rise
stark against the skyline.
Well that's OK, to so mark
your place, your past so long
as you don't go hanging
anything on them.

And it's a bleak day out there, the sea ominous, the sand
    irongrey and the sky greyer,
and the bush leached of its green/gone black and bronze
    where mist and spume
let it be seen

light a fire
        light a fire
                and a tired ghost under the gorse hedge
                grumbling at having to go already

let me tell you sadness
let me tell you woes

let me talk of madness
because that's the way it goes, the world
that's the way it goes

o my love, there are lean hammer-headed clouds
menacing us from the horizon
and red-eyed moths beating on the doors

and the kettle, snoring away on the hob

'You would not know just by looking
but under that corner of my lawn
is the corpse of a shining cuckoo
which, in ecstatic prospect of the Bismarck archipelago,
failed to notice my window — and there
lies nextdoor's cat after mauling once too long
once too often/my home fantails one May morning, and
under here I buried the remains of my heart —
o, the potatoes? Like the sunchokes they
are self-sown — well, at least I never planted *them* — yes
it is a green well-nourished lawn.'

                    The house-cricket is winter-drowsy
                    and the spiders are moving in
                    but zitzit zitzit zitzit
                    until this gig is done

Objects taken in
become intrajects.

We are all taken in.

Can I wind my voice into your ear
and around your heart? O yes
I can, because your eyes let me
let me in —

My house lies
equidistant between Antarctica and Australia:
I can't hear a call from either
but a thousand miles a thousand years away
a wave rises in Hawaiki-nui Hawaiki-pamamao
and breaks here

on the rocks in the dark, the rocks at the far end
are fat with mussels: select some dozens
and steal them away.
Young shellfish, I scrape you so easily out of your shells . . . aue!
so rich with the possibilities of life! Ka tangi ahau with tears of steam
but it's just a shame and your damnation you taste soo sweet
    — and these extras,
peacrabs tucked in the soft security of mussel mantle;
   peacrabs loaded
with ochre-red eggs, taste a bit gritty but taste pretty good, as
   does a sea-spider
couched away here in the steamed mantle erstwhile cool home,
the little toil now still
of chitonous candy-glass legs, crunch. Ah well, we all
should make such sweetness, such douce noise at our going

'the sea hath fish for everyone'

        and so it is:

                What luck!
                A hen-crab, in berry
                and me with pot and appetite
                just sitting here
                ready!

A Taoist sage-of-the-beaches
supplementing the chancy gifts
with seaweed
and sad mutants that crawl ashore

. . . o they shout in chorus
                    stick her in the iron pot
                    try her out —

I go fishing with spiders
I go fishing with flies
sometimes I catch fish but
there is more to fishing than catching

the cloud of terns glitters blacks flickers glints as they wheel
foil and white wing and dark cap and reel

                    so the bush is grey, grey the lake
                    and the hills retreating greyly
                    from the eyes
                    and the rain falls unceasingly
                    from grey and sodden skies
                    while the steely bladed flax
                    flexes and shines with/unholy sparking pride

the drone of days coming
                    going going

and the black brooding bulls in Flanagan's paddocks

and the still white bird at the water's edge

                    •oOo•

Who are these strangers
walking my beach?
Grey as the mists, shrouded
in heavy cowled coats/they carry
rods but do not fish the sea:
they confer in huddles of three;
my guardian shivers, wood creaking in the damp.
I can see no faces and the kaitiaki's paua eyes
go pale.

15

Here comes the rain again.
Night is drawing in.
The roaring of a hard sea, and next day
the sand of the strand alive with tumble-suds, sea-froth —

She had travelled twenty thousand miles
to hear an answer to her question
'Was the child real?'

She could have sent a letter
but then, we would not have so
voluptuously consumed
the avocados
the champagne —

to make her feel better
I add,
'The child, one way or the other,
travelled even further'
and that, for her for me,
that truth is real.

MAPS FOR THE UNWARY
For a long time there
in everything I wrote
I was throwing salt over my shoulder
breadcrumbs for a small ghost
who's grown and gone now
I hope

but watch out: there's a chameleon here, practising shadows.
Here, I call, here. Hear! (I'm calling you) hear!
Hea? Hea? O life is hard enough without all these homophones
flying round my ears.

I don't tell lies. I just don't tell the truth, all the truth, just
some of the truth mulched with clichés, and all clichés have
a nub of truth; even much-tongued things are very faintly
potent, like old old ambergris.

> I have a stone that once swam
> strange warm ancient seas.
> Do not chide me, saying
> You have swapped the stark clarity of crystal
> for the opal's shifty indefinities
> blue no green no
> water caught and held/fossilised made lively
> winking stone.
> It is the jester's truth,
> lead crystal makes me sick and this
> is a water world.

Three pigeons come and
perching in my peppermint gum
commence to whistle their wings.

Between the sight
and the sound
of a word
is silence:
no telling
what will come
out of it.

> There was one afternoon, all mingled Rangoon oil and boronia:
> I'd been cleaning the guns, and a friend brought in the flowers
> — he grows older and thinner
> but his eyes now stay steady on my face —
> it was a pungent and delicious to the nose day, somehow reminiscent
> of fine aromatic tobacco. We talk of death
> as usual, and then he takes his cancer home.

Another dark winter-day, and my fingers are numb and water-shrunk,
self shrivelled and withered with the cold, yet
inside I am as clean as that surf-scoured rock,
no compassion left for anything.

       The numbered days flicker past/so fast so fast so fast

I go away: I come back: the heron is nowhere
to be seen

ZAZEN

Pihareinga
it is three in the morning:
do you think
continuing your song
into this utter dark
will bring you to nirvana
before the dawn?

I had longed for that liquid chirruping so many mistake for
  birds at night
— the treefrogs are singing Rain Rain — and
for the periodic creak of trees nestled into the side of my house and
the never-ceasing omnipresent Tasman surf
       that endless song that soothes
       smoothes the sudden angularities
       of morepork sheep and human crying
and for the brush of rain from a swiftly passing sou'west shower
changing to near-quiet, allowing in
the cold-drowsy greet of a cricket, and
kettle and range making a chorus

but my head is ringing with the talk from a rowdy midnight pub;
he had wanted company, they said, ever since she died he had wanted
and at last it could stand the calling no longer;
it clothed itself in any rag, tatters of fur from longdead possum

felted into the road; a shred of greened cloth from bones the
    sea had exposed;
it snatched flesh from whatever made itself handy, rotting or
    freshfallen,
cell-life just fled: clumsy and hurting, it wove itself a larynx
and a tongue from the moaning wind, and gathered eyes of
    foam and glow-worm shine.
The hair he said he loved was easiest: it seized the toetoe's
    worn winter plumes.
It shambled, desperate but not despairing, now locked into
    the rubbish golem,
and thus, terribly, his hunger and his need came to him.

          Listen
          it is rattling out there in the dark
          trying to sing in a voice that lacks tact
          knows only the need:
          let you
          let me in —

My friend Flanagan finally dies.
They put his bulls down.
Mad buggers, wouldn't let you near them,
says the gun man. Thanks for the tea.

Tuia tuia, tui tui a —
there are needles enough
shuttling backwards and forth
making the pattern
that is also the teacher

        'Arise and drink your bliss, for everything that lives
          is holy.'

William Blake, you knew it all
and nothing of this world,
sipping sour wine,
watching a sea —

There are more things under my roof
than I want there to be.
The maps are clouds, and reading
clouds is a late-developing skill.

On the fence-lines the waxeyes
plump from my compost pit
are huddled, green and thankful and still.

·o◯o·

I walk by night I walk by day I am walking my life away —

the stick I carry is manuka, trimmed and smoked and oiled
to a dark red smoothness. It is easy in my hand,
heavy, dependable: there are three small spirals
unwinding into each other in a frieze round its top.

I clasp my hands, over the spirals, over each other and
watch the birds turning in the sky. Their tangi
is distant: the heron hunched on my fence does not reply.

Feel the mud under your toes. Feel this deep warm inviting
mud — no shells or sharp things to harm your skin — just a
squelching friendly mud. Just a easeful welcoming mud.
Protective mud. In the beginning, there was mud. In this
end, mud.

### Lines For A Listening Drowned Body

Don't they know
how voices travel over water?

'She's not here she's
            not here.'

But I am, I am down among the new green reeds
ready for spring, and the sticks here have ceased to prickle
my ribs, and the mud is warming up — even the crabs
have grown used to me, up this ivory reef and scuttle
into the sockets and — jacks all — waving red claws
are softened into dancing sprightly gavottes
to the music in this sphere

       — can't they hear?

Against sunset bracken turns blackly lacy
and toetoe to fine funereal feathers
even gorse makes a delicate tracery
                   — you forget the dust and scratch and spike
in these silhouettes, and quietly marvel:
it's like Earth seen from Moon
a most marvellous cloud-laced bluegreen globe
and not a ballooning hunger-belly
or bruised face in sight.

It's slack moon, neap water, black moon, too quiet for anything
but brooding.

'Drink seawater with the moon,' she said, a brown woman
smelling strongly of the fire's smoke. 'Not a lot, for your body
will not stand a lot. Drink the tide from the new moon, drink
the tide with the waxing moon, drink the tide until the full
moon comes round. Then, drink sweetwater while it wanes.
Good for your body, good for your mind.'
'And for your soul,' he said, a little dark man who never told
anyone much, 'stand in the tideway an hour after. Remember:
consider: dream.'

       The first time
       it seemed to shine
       more moon in the water
       than there was moon in the sky.

The heron in moonlight
stops my heart: too white too white
the rest of the bird/the best of the bird is listening
in the dim of that strange house
where the carvings flicker and dance
and the singing of worlds winds through all words.

The rafts of foam drift in, float further up and further on:
tonight the setting sun has armoured them
in crustacean colours, redbrown with angry shadows.
I know they come from the sea, cities and estates of diatoms:
they seem to have an end in sight, there is deliberation in
    their journeying,
are strangely martial, buoyed-up forts held by numberless silent ranks
of creatures who can compose cliffs and plateaux after death.
I know where they come from but not where they go,
have met them at a watery kind of carfax,
have patrolled with them up the dark lagoon,
but the wind whittles away a squad there, a battalion here,
and they sneak into tribulets where my kayak cannot follow —
there is probably something more important I should be doing,
than chasing bubbles.

I must stop dreaming, I must stop gleaning
the paper-winged mantic phrase that drifts so lazily down the mind —

Reality is important: reality is more important: reality is
most important.

                    (There are no goblins elves or piskies
                    infiltrating reality here —
                    just this solitary taniwha
                    thoughtfully picking her teeth
                    (staring at the sea
                    wondering where
                    the next whirlpool
                    should be) )

## A Practical Alternative To Insect Sprays
### (as told by Kerry Crump)

No, she said seriously, not just any moths. Those slow fat
porinas — why bother, eh? Nobody'd seriously call that
sport. No, it was only those fancy ones, little delta-winged
jobs. Nifty miniature buggers blitzing to and fro — *those*
ones, they were wortha bullet, eh?

Bullet? Bullet!

Weelllllll . . . she stuffed her pipe during the pause. Well,
actually, we invented the original .000177. Didn't have to
breathe too hard on your ammo, eh. And, once inserted in
the breech, it didn't go bang. Not even pop. More like (tiny
tiny wee letters) phft. And the moths twitched and stopped
mid-shimmy and sorta spiralled down to the carpet. Not very
spectacular, truth being told. Moth shootin' never did catch
on much.

The pieces of petrified sea on her fingers wink at us.

But shit o dear, the wasp-shotguns!

> (Leave us alone with our story
> leave us alone
> do not tamper with the way it might have been.)

The heron hunches on my roof at night.
The heron hunches on my fence in the day.

If this was anywhere else I would be worried by the presence,
   by the stillness.
But he isn't any kind of aitua: he has just finished spearing
   the daily ration

of waxeyes in the Chatham Islands olearia, fishing the bush
    like he was fishing
an upriver pool.

There was one tauhou preternaturally wary and,
    somehow, knowing;
as yet another bird was jabbed and defeathered while
    shrilling despair
it would whistle a single sad pipe.
It is the counter of kin-dead? The flock-heart? The one who is aware?

It happens, it happens — this morning just after dawn
I watch an old ewe wake: she heaves herself to her feet
and stands with her head hanging, ground whitefrozen by her muzzle.
She sighs (I see the sigh) and shudders. Her fleece
    ripples with the shudder.
Another goddamned day of chewing frozen grass. And
    the end of it is —
She straddles her back legs and pees crystal on the
    grass, shakes her head.
Then sheeplike, sheeplike again, wanders away.

The seasons are:
a glean of herrings, a swarm of eels,
a creel of 'bait and a siege of herons.
Come summer
            all will pass.

My home is invaded by another joker, thin as a blade with a
bare torso. She grins through her skull. Her curls hide her
eyes. She holds out her hands and shadows dance on her
palms, and a pair of tiny owls, the size of porina moths,
whizz round her head shrieking, 'World's smallest birds!' They
hoot with strigine laughter. 'World's smallest! Gangway!
Scram!' She is the Spice Merchant, and she dresses in a
careful kilt of grey silk. She carries her goods in strange
boxes made from huon pine or kauri gum, hollow-out fossil

crabs or bloated tropic shells stoppered with wax, all held in
a net of music. She sells threads of saffron macerated in
tears, and aromatic narcotic ambers, and much much more
exotic wares.
'We're shadow-merchants, you and I. Liars, like cooks and physicists.'
No, we both deal in echoes, I reply.
I trade her a soul and
I choose the wine.
I choose the wine.

There's a new moon tugging this tide
urgently upriver:
watch her rouse and swell
and burst the bulrush border — watch her now
over she comes!
fleet fleet fast towards you —

It's been Welcome! the rich feasts of winter
pink flesh of smoked eels, the tangy succulence of oysters,
muttonbirds grilled so their skin crackles and the sweet fat bastes
the kumara, the baked yams, the wrinkled salmon-pink yams,
and the tongue is tingled by a quintessential southern salad
pale cabbage and the glory of tamarillo — such shared feasts
lap these curves these sturdy bones with another inch of warmth
against the leaner spring —

so let us dance          let us dance

let us dream a tauhou: the mossgreen back, greyish breast
    and russet flanks;
the matchstick legs that can look pink, and the bright white-
    rimmed eyes.
A flick-quick yet plump little bird, seeming all feathers and squeak,
driven in winter by the fire in its belly
— must eat      must eat      must eat —
even after I cease composing the pit by the olearia tree
they visit, full of hunger and twittering hope

let us dance        let us dance

but who can dance with the shades?
Who can dance/without a head?
— the music is no matter —

It can stand leant forward, dagger beak poised
so intent you hold your breath, so long you gulp air
and lose it and wait breathless again
the heron is not real, the heron is carved, an S-curve, immobile
it must topple a wind eddy will the moment is forever
the stab is faster        than vision
blurs even a camera's eye
the strangers see it coming
and dodge into thin air
except the one, the eyed, the paralysed,
that which is pierced and briskly shaken
from its skin and gulped
raw and squeaking still

sometimes the heron will commence to sway
a slow slow side-to-side sinuosity
and a hypnotised tauhou joins this deadly reel
feet glued to branch and minute shaking head full
of fixed and rigid eye

as it dies
they panic for a moment distressing the air
they settle a moment later
the heron waits, a moment.

The world turns
the moon grows
old in its light
and at last the toetoe
let loose their creamygreen hair;
the kamahi is rowdy with flowers
one great & buzzing inflorescence

blooming Spring Spring Spring.
I can put a kettle on just to brew content:
the sun shines, baby spiders float by
on their natal silks,
an early cuckoo calls kui kui a —

> And what if we are the exceptions
> and now the exceptional time?
> That before it was always gentle summer
> and the fish always stranded
> and after long full lives
> people always died in their sleep
> smiling?

Raking over the compost pit, a cockleshell a cabbage stalk
  an ivory fragile skull
(a head shook off this far) a cockleshell: I strew gravel for remembrance.
  I shall plant another olearia
  a windbreak      shelter
  guardian against hunchbacks on the fence —

  Without rock, how can I tell water?
  Sunshine is meaningless without grey weather
  and what is joy without knowledge of pain?

> The heron is flying
> back home again
> past the sunset past the night
> into the light immensity —

Evening:
the dandelions and hawkbit
are folded shut

no wind

and the sea barely curling
on the strand

## 2

# AGAINST
# THE SMALL EVIL VOICES

---

Sometimes, if you listen too carefully, you hear things:

parangeki buzzing above, indicators of disaster,
puwawau, aitua heard in running water,
tupaoe, which (they say) are spirits singing at night, for no
   good reason —
irewaru, same sort of beast, overheard only on the coasts,
and the ill-omened ororua, humming busily through the air —

personally, while I have heard all these ill-luck chanters
in grey and depressed times, I know the worst kind live
in the city, in the suburbs, where each hutch is nearly
insulated by the white noise of TV against
the nextdoor screams.

> I have listened for a life
> to voices on the wind
> they keep calling
> there is no end —
> but the wind blowing
> begins again
> & in the mind
> cries like a knife

Ah, sweet life, We share it
with cancers and tapeworms
with bread moulds and string beans
and great white sharks . . .

I am not a person to say the words out loud
I think them strongly, or let them hunger from the page:
know it from there, from my silence, from somewhere other
than my tongue

        the quiet love
        the silent rage

# PAPATUANUKU E TU!

My mother is a young woman
            my mother is young
she has seen a thousand summers and their springs
            and as they come
and go she laughs, o my mother sings
and cries and brings another running on.

My mother is forty-one cycles and aged and hopeless
— no, hoping for some fierceness before surcease
rather than to be always the water child —
that my mother is me — then again
my mother has swung through a thousand thousand great cycles
she is the Albatross and has
all chicks under her wings

and my mother has already swum through
                        the endless seas drumming
time, the while, return, the beginning, to end
and she is commencing swimming again

my mother breathes every breath
you breathe    I breathe    them all/others
with us/without    she has us under her skin
swarming and on her skin warming
all the world yea even unto the volcano's lip.

She slips easily, my mother
into the courtesy of variety:
black as coral she sings
and white as coral sands sun-fused
and that odd lovely pink&yellow coral can be
although my mother's blood is green as chlorophyll
and she is cloaked in the three awesome blues —

I tangi I call I am aching because
I cannot hymn her with more
than brief finally silent words

        whom I breathe
        who breathes me

and it is insufficient to sing
'Hear the moths ride the cinnamon breezes
and in the groaning echolalic abyss
the whale songs ring'

        I breathe
        who breathes me
        who breathes not least
        of all, thee

e darkling,
who said in the shadows

        'After us, everything —'

# TE RUA HAEROA O TE TOKOTORU

Dig me a pit in the cold clay
dig me a pit
let them eat earth
let them eat it, eat it
prisoned so their skulls flatten
prisoned so their spines crack
and wormlike they delve forever
toward the flaming heart of Her
who waits, with infinite patience,
for them to arrive

    the rapists the bandits
    the arrogant men stripping the seas
    contemplating with cool hearts
    the incandescent dust
    of a murdered planet.
    Dig that pit!
    Hasten them in —

Make no mistake — gods are alive
are awake, and they walk the earth
of our hearts: their footsteps are called
many names indivisible from One, and to say
She is ours
is to be a child with an apple
a girl in a walled garden chanting
I have the world

o sisters listen —

The Three are on the strand
all evening their talk comes in drifts
not easy to stand, to understand:
there is a thin fragile fingernail edge of moon,

a wind off the sea.
They crouch round their triple-handled cup
it is ever-brimming
now with water which comes in all the colours of human eyes
now with tea, steam cruising the amber/the jadey top
now with the bloodrich wine.

The mother has put down her skin bag of babies
the skin is swirling water and a smoky coil of tears
she croons over the myriad children
she presses her nose to each and they gurgle and sneeze and smile
she breathes light into them and they lift aloft
like bubbles, and like bubbles vanish,
she is singing the while.

        Dig me a pit in the red earth
        dig me a pit that they may sleep
        let them sleep
        the beaten the infibulated
        the spirit-broken/the girl who
        chewed the stitches out of her wrists
        to bleed to death    this time

the starved mothers holding starved babies to starved breasts
and those whose care and giving has worn them
to grey wraithes of staring eyes & patience and
the petrol-soaked women

        let them sleep.

The mother drinks bloody wine and a handle mists away
and the old old woman snorts and tosses back her ragged white curls
she drinks iron water and keeps firm grip on the cup
and her black eyes glitter as she says, There are harder songs
   to be sung
harder, she insists on that ancient hardness, not just sleep
Sleep! she spits, that comes to everyone, earth stars and you,

even you and your ever-changing self-same brood — have you noticed
they keep coming back full of heartbruises and tears?
Why bother sending them out any more?

Go teach your granny to suck eggs, snaps the mother
and the old lady cackles
in the most resonant and evil way
and from her own soul and snot and saliva
blows an amazing isinglass globe
aglow with promise and yolky radiance
and she winks
and smacks her lips
and sucks it dry
and sniggers
and throws the brittle emptied world away
and snakes off over the windtorn sand howling
with heartless laughter —

> Dig me that pit
> to put the shit in
> a piece of skin a hair
> will do/then I've got them
> gutted castrated weighted down
> by their own names
> deep in the dung
> where they belong — I've got you!
> she shrieks, I've got you!
> and here is the pit.

*Never* tell your granny to go suck eggs:
she's off to do a larger one —

There is one handle left on the cup:
the mother sighs and takes her ever-moving ever-fecund sac
and as she goes, she beckons
and the girl from the garden comes closer
she is young and old and wise as the new tide

she is not human
she cannot help seeing
that even a mountain is a dance:
she stares at the world and the empty strand
with feral indigo eyes,
and laughter is far from her, she does not know tears:
she snaps her teeth together,
scrabbles a pit in the watery sand
and whispers names over the raw edge five million
million names whispered to die in the silence —


                    listen:
                    there is nothing
                    there is only/the wind from the sea

# LULLABY FOR A STONE DOLL

O I could suck on their brains!
Those long-tongued spiteful men!

Their lewd words
rob me of my place
I am footloose on a barren way
searching for something lost
never mind! I shall be all parents to you —
here, a plaited cover, a cloak to keep you from the cold
like any other winterborn child,
muka to protect that raw new navel and titoki oil
and I shape you, with caress, as any massaging mother does
    her soft newborn
hah! but that will teach them to jeer
Hine-i-turama my highborn self —

I'll charge you with so much love
that you'll laugh
and cry real tears
and I will hear your heartbeat
ticking away like a small cicada
at night.

And I even have a name for you, son —
Tuwairua
— do you like it?
We shall be able to say our names together
when we go down to the dark,
you and I.

They say I am mad
I am made I am mad but
I dwell secure on earth
under any sky

and care for all I have wrought —
whatever you are, baby,
you are safe with me —

what am I afraid of?
Not that mixture of fist and tongue they thrust out
but of hurting without comfort without surcease
even after the dark
forgetting to care being hopeless
the eel to get my heartmeat is despair

but still I hold you
with love —

O I could eat them!


*This poem is indebted to a patere (chant with gestures, and
frequently of an abusive nature) composed by Hine-i-turama,
an aristocrat of Ngati Rangiwewehi. She composed her song
when she was accused of being pregnant — she was a puhi (a
chiefly woman who was supposed to remain a virgin until an
arranged marriage which would bring honour to her people
was accomplished). She made herself a stone baby and sang
the patere in derision of her accusers. However, it is also
recorded that she really did have a baby, Tuwairua, and
composed the patere in defiance. Hine-i-turama's patere can be
found in* Nga Moteatea, *collected by A. T. Ngata, and translated
by P. Te H. Jones, part II, page 111 (Polynesian Society, 1961).
This poem was originally exhibited in* Mothers *at the Women's
Gallery, Wellington, 1981, with two accompanying drawings.*

# HE HOHA

Bones tuned, the body sings —

See me,
I am wide with swimmer's muscle, and a bulk and luggage I
    carry curdled on hips;
I am as fat-rich as a titi-chick, ready for the far ocean flight.

See me,
I have skilled fingers with minimal scars, broad feet that
    caress beaches,
ears that catch the music of ghosts, eyes that see the
    landlight, a pristine womb
untouched except by years of bleeding, a tame unsteady heart.

See me,
I am a swamp, a boozy brain with stinking breath, a sour
sweatened flesh;
I am riddled with kidneyrot, brainburn, torn gut, liverfat,
scaled with wrinkles,
day by day I am leached, even between smiles, of that
strange water, electricity.

See me,
I am my earth's child,

    and she, humming
    considers her cuts and scars, and debates our death.
    Mean the land's breast, hard her spine when turned against you;
    jade her heart.

Picture me a long way from here —
back bush, a rainbird calling,
the sea knocking shore.

41

It is a cliché that once a month, the moon stalks through my body,
rendering me frail and still more susceptible to brain spin;
it is truth that cramp and clot and tender breast beset — but then
it is the tide of potency, another chance to walk through the
    crack between worlds.

What shall I do when I dry, when there is no more turning
    with the circling moon?
Ah, suck tears from the wind, close the world's eye;
Papatuanuku still hums.

But picture me a long way from here.

    Waves tuned, the mind-deep sings —

    She forgot self in the city, in the flats full of dust and
        spider-kibbled flies;
    she forgot the sweetness of silence in the rush and roar
        of metal nights;
    no song fitted her until she discovered her kin, all
        swimmers in the heavy air of sea;

    she had lost the supple molten words, the rolling thunder,
    the night hush of her mother's tongue;
    she had lost the way home, the bright road, the trodden
        beach, the mewling gulls,
    the lean grey toe of land.
    In the lottery of dreams, she gained prize of a
        nightmare, a singular dark.

But picture her a long way from there,
growing quiet until she heard herself whispered by the sea on
    the blackest night,
and echoed in the birds of morning.

    Keening, crooning, the untuned spirit —

I am a map of Orion scattered in moles across this
    firmament of body;
I am the black hole, the den where katipo are busy spinning
    deadhavens,
and he won't go, the cuckoo child.
Jolted by the sudden thud and shatter, I have gone outside to find
the bird too ruffled, too quiet, the barred breast broken, an
    end of the far travelling.

Tutara-kauika, you father of whales, you servant of Tangaroa,
your little rolling eye espies the far traveller — quick!
whistle to him, distract, send him back to the other island;
I don't mind ever-winter if summer's harbinger is so
    damaged, damaging.

He turned full to face me, with a cry to come home —
do you know the language of silence, can you read eyes?

When I think of my other bones, I bleed inside,
and he won't go, the cuckoo-child.

It is not born; it is not live; it is not dead;
it haunts all my singing, lingers greyly, hates and hurts and
    hopes impossible things.
And Papatuanuku is beginning her ngeri, her anger is growing
thrumming in quakes and tsunami,

and he won't go, the cuckoo's child.

        O, picture me a long way from here;
        tune the bones, the body sings;
    quiet the mind, the spirit hums,
        and Papatuanuku trembles, sighs;
        till then among the blood and dark
        the shining cuckoo spreads its wings
        and flies this hoha, this buzz and fright,
        this wave and sweat and flood,
        this life.

# DEITY CONSIDERED AS MOTHER DEATH

Now,
night is menace, mystery,
no handhold here
changes the redmist dawning daughter to someone beyond laughter
poised as a spider,
her doorkeepers, shadows.

Her children now
the baby children of death
the bandylegged potbellied slanteyed bonechests
and the shrinking ghosts wrapped in Her night hair.

(Have you noticed the skull
that hides under your skin
caging your mind?)

She
guards over our dreams of living, soothes our songs our whimpering
waits for the blooming of that instinct
that draws us into traps of flame like light
sends us out moths again
waits
never smiles

                    Her privates, they say
                    are bladed with flakes of blackstone
                    sharper than grief.
                    Her eyes, they say
                    are blank and jade.
                    Her skin still skin of the Girla Dawn
                    but intruded on by shadows and
                    such careless shapes as the body assumes on dying.
                    Her hair, they say
                    flowing tangling closing as seaweed

over your head after Rerenga-wairua
they say.

From the Lady of Clay the Girla Dawn first wakened
red and smiling

                                        nobody asks to be born
                                        nobody asks to be born

We all share being
born of blood and water
dying
going from dark to dark

So we began
dreaming swimmers on inward seas
and live and die —
why death after being? why being? why death?
Come, let us go and ask our mother together
hand in hand to the door
ask Her poised in her shadow, Hinenuitepo —

Did you not often ask
the unanswerable questions of your mother?
And did she not
answer you?

*This poem was also exhibited, with a drawing, in* Mothers *at
the Women's Gallery in 1981.*

# PAUASHELL GODS

It was the year of omens
> dead dolphin on the Watercup Beach
> oil slick flexing with each wave
> by Fisherman's Reef

> > Maukiekie brooded
> > shagridden as ever.

> > From what island
> > does the seaweed come?

It was a season of strut and strangeness
hurt, crippledness, too sudden changes,
the year of our pauashell gods.

And I know growing up is called
many other names.

> > Now the kelp
> > is in its golden breeding colours;
> > now the gulls
> > court and preen, beg and skirl
> > and scream and shag each other.
> > It is the ripe moonwater month,
> > open fecundity
> > I had never noticed before.

It is the children believing another child
whistling as he breathed — no change or strangeness
in that: legs locked
neatly into place, smile screwed
like a pain-line on his face,
the perfect puppet with the perfect mask.

You don't know when it's good, he said,
you don't even know when it's bad.
Nobody's tweezed your shell off yet,
nobody's woke your ghosts.

Hear us laugh.

> Now the mating trees
> send yellowgrit eggs
> down the wind.

He held the nacred shell
— Jesus and Mary and God my arse,
I can make this do lightnings —
and grinned for the devil in his soul.

> Now the sea
> is full of summer thunder
> summer rain and green ghost wildfire
> over the whale-hump hills.

Pauashell gods have no names,
they take a lot of finding:
when you set them up
do not seek answers.
All they do is listen
and, occasionally,
shake your world.

Sacrifice?
— it was my proud word —
We don't make no sacrifice,
they take their sacrifice.

Sometimes his grin bleached his face.

Dried cod, mouth still paining from the hook,
hanging in the north wind,
even a wet south tomorrow
will bring no relief.

I had never noticed before.

An earshell, listening ...
we dreamed of towers and powers and lightnings
so, children being rats in the adult world,
we stole in and stole glue and stole out
before they knew they were plundered.

(That still boatshed, held exact until now in memory,
reels and creels and kelpbags
cordage and floats and broken oars
rusted tins with rust-shut lids
and old old hooks.)

We glued gross round idols, all ears
to catch the whisper of the world;
shining sea totems that cupped the power of waves;
he bound maimed shells to make a vulnerable god.

Now it is good to know a god decays
bit by bit, scraped by insect wind or sea
into oblivion, like us, but then
all the words were, The more holes,
the more ears — mine's the wisest.

                              Did they hear?
                              And from what island
                              does the seaweed come?

Never start believing your own myths.
We are a cruel though inventive race.

Now the golden scum
of kelp seeds and rots and dies;
now the gulls
have sailed down the wind
to rocks of home.
I have swallowed pollen.
Suppose it grows little trees
in the head?

The altar is within a shallow cave
the anthem is always the roll of the sea.
The adults are glad of our absence.
The aimless arrow cometh.

We developed a war with another beach tribe
who created a mocking race of crab godlets:
ambush and kidnap and inquisition
and jeering cries to recant —
they sailed the days of that summer away
until it all turned serious and they shat on our altar
and smashed our gods with lewd stones.

Their laughter, beating down the cliff
like a rockfall.
We hope they die soon.
Or maybe, maybe, seeing they're paua
a giant foot of gluey dark, he said,
to cap them and suck their skulls dry.

I liked the image.
It was the year I discovered science fiction.

And it was drums when Soph broke her leg by the cliff
and trumpets when they took Tahu to Borstal

and an abyss
when our strange prophet vanished.

Take a paua shell
run your finger over
that roughened scar where muscle clenched
and grew and failed — know well
we all lose the sea war —

We never learned where he went:
the adults merely stopped talking
except to say, Go play outside,
and the other gang said, Ask your gods.

I have never learned where he went:
it's one of those small mysteries
which returns with the tide of years
(we are not speaking of someone important
for his head was always away with the birds:
Hey I'm not broken, am I?
No: bent is all.)

It is the want of answers:

                              from what island
                              did the seaweed come?

            Now the kelp
            waves black and winter-sinister;
            now the gulls
            hunch one-legged against the wind;
            now the trees
            bend and bow and moan.

The only survival is to hold on
to all you know,
or burrow deeper into the dark —
the paua still has lessons.

I last saw them
left glittering dust in the crevice
shrouded by seaweed:
they may still be there

anyway, for Pipi
who never trusted his own shadow
here is one
and
here is one
and
here is one

*This poem, with an accompanying pauashell god and four
painted panels, was part of the opening exhibition of the
Women's Gallery, Wellington, 1980.*

# WAITING ON THE LAUGHING OWL

It is a good night for watching
steady moon/lake mirroring light
stern trees rearing skyward
(hazy) and backing limestone cliffs
ripe with little crevices and holes wherein
might hide the last laughing owl
— hear old authors/longdead listeners talk back from books:
'a bray like a jackass'
'a kicked dog, a whipped pup'
'a scream to raise
horripilation'
(a right conjurer that last one) —
anyway we are huddled under a blanket
admiring the surround
not cold as the fire reaches for the moon
whispering, taking a suck
at the whisky flask, waiting
on the laughing owl to show
itself anew:
it grows towards morning/stillness
a fish kisses the watertop
the ripples spread to here —
all is stainless quiet
except
that stupid bird shrieking whekau! whekau!
but as soon as dawn has wrung its neck
we will regain peace and light will come
waiting on the laughing owl

# 3

## SOME WINESONGS

O, I was born old and
I was born sad and
I was born bold
to sing those things
that had to be said —

I will sing a lovesong
— do not hide your ears
it is time for heartsongs and it is time for tears —
lady, I am a lover
lady, I am a thief
and I need your heart, love
as I need wine and tide and beach —

I will sing a tidesong
to while away your fears
you will hear the sea sound, you will hear deep prayers
but lady, I am a loner
and truly, I am a thief
and I will keep your heart-love
within my bottle's reach

and take it out in moonlight
and finger it with awe
until mazed with night caresses
I'll praise the bottle more.

When I sing this winesong
you'd better stop your ears
it only brings you emptiness
and strange and hopeless cares —

# THE BOND OF BEES

I'm blending my mind
with the ease of wine
from candle flowers
on a warm afternoon
and a bloom of bees
from the kamahi
resounds    resounds
in the quiet room

        spikes to the honey
        bees to the comb
        the yeast to the sweet mead
        and now the mead home

# THE WINE-RICH ARTERIES

The rain is falling in my head
it lilts the rhythm of the dead
            haere haere ki te po
the rain is falling in my heart

the sun is shining in my mind
it blinds the memories that I find
            haere haere ki te po
the sun is burning up my heart

the wind is blowing in my bones
it tries to dry the sap to stone
            haere haere ki te po
      it seeks the wine-rich arteries
      all the sweet and pulsing parts
      all the debris of my heart
and whines to set them free:
whistle, wind, for futility
            haere haere ki te po

# SING IT ROUND THE PYRE

If I
go down to Death tonight
cry:
with long sounds and songs of mourning, or out with loud
    words of glee
then,
light a fire on the beach for me.

You can set the flames with rejoicing smiles
as easily as with grief
and all the difference is
knowledge, or belief

                    have a care for the sparks meanwhile

# WINESONG FOR THE WICKED IN RETIREMENT

— but Hole-In-The wall was so cold, my dear!
Hole-In-The-Wall is so cold

and outlaws have lost their zing, my dear
outlaws are not so bold —

so we're left with this friendly port
my love
to warm the waiting night.
It's all red go no green left my love
and no need to show another light,
above, my dear
below

There is a name I use in the daytime
and a name I use at night
names for walking on the left side
names for trampling down the right.

                Pass the bottle, lady.

I have a name I use at the tideline
and another for swimming in the sea
and one for when I'm landbound
and several for flying free.

                Pass the bottle, lady,
                observe the level of the wine.

I have a name I am called in my living
and a secret one waiting for death
a name for the time I am breathing
and a last name for the last breath.

                Pass the bottle, lady,
                observe the level of the wine —
                time flows slowly, lady.

Names from friends and lovers
names from enemies
names in war and fighting
and names in peace:
I have one name here before me
another to leave behind,
and not one name fits all me
not any name in time —

Pass the bottle, lady,
observe the level of the wine;
time flows slowly, lady —
all down the line
and what name would you give me?

# WINESONG 27

All your passions
matched to mine
are as ebbtide matched to flood
are as water matched to blood
are vinegar to wine.

      And yet
      betimes surprised
      by elusive shining fish
      amongst the coral of your mind
      I hesitate to break and wait
      to find

            all your passions
            matched to mine
            are as ebbtide matched to flood
            are as water matched to blood
            are vinegar to wine.

# ANTIDOTES TO MINDRUSH

There is a copper bell chiming
there is
a windfish flying
there is
all the sea rising —
but consider
beyond these
the still island in its seas
and calm of hills

# OLD OLD WINESONG

Of purple leather my purse is made
and lined with silk and silver
I bury my dead on a wooden sled
held down by a long jade cover
and I wander the road the sea has laid
all the wide world over

# SAYING NOTHING/IN THE END
## (Lines to be put on a gravestone)

E, wrap me in the black bark cloth
                                    strew kokowai
and let there be white bones
                                    between my teeth
                                    (fish or birds, god knows
                                    and I'll no longer care)
and a paua-hafted hook
laid handily
to show my trade


                            — catching dreams —


and poenemu
(just to own
I loved, and lived,
and loved the stone).
                                    Aue, taukiri e!
                                    Here's to the beautiful ones
                                    who got away!